AUSTRALIA?

AUSTRALIA?

Know Before You Go!

Martin Dean Tobin

To order additional copies of this book, contact:
Xlibris
1-800-455-039
www.Xlibris.com.au
Orders@Xlibris.com.au
723325

CONTENTS

INTRO / DISCLAIMER

As the author, I must admit that many of the observations herein are very much my own rather subjective, and at times rather cynical commentary, based largely on my own personal experience, much of which i'd rather forget. However, I believe that many of life's most valuable lessons and insights are not always the most pleasant ones. So I still think they can be useful to anyone thinking of travelling to Oz, or moving there for any reason. And in any case, I hope they make interesting reading.

I have put the more serious points in bold print, and the less serious ones are not in bold.

As time goes on, some of the facts and details herein are bound to become out-of-date. Nonetheless, most of what I write will remain at least relatively true, probably as long as there is a big hot southern land called Australia.

LANGUAGE WARNING. When Aussies open their mouths wide enough to say something clearly, it's usually an expletive or two. So, to make this book as true-to-life as possible, I have included occasional swear-words, Aussie slang and dry humour.

MY PERSPECTIVE. I've written this little bit to disarm those boring people who assert things like "Everything depends on your perspective!", as if that's some revolutionary new discovery, or some profound insight. Well my perspective is this: I was born in Sydney, whether I liked it or not – and basically, I don't! And I'm writing this book largely to come to terms with Australia for once and for all, and to put it behind me to move somewhere else. If you want to know what a place is really like, instead of reading glossy brochures and talking to travel-agents, you can often learn much more from people who <u>don't</u> like it, and finding out why! Yes, it's a contrarian approach, and it works. So while I have tried to make this book somewhat humourous, it also tells you the hot, hard facts.

WHY THIS BOOK? To expose Australia for the popular lie that it really is – for once and for all! Many people travel to Australia and even migrate there without even knowing much about it – with some naïve idea that it's a sunny paradise where they can make a fast fortune, and then dash off back to their home country after a year or two. <u>This is a very common and very costly mistake!</u>

Once you're there, if you then decide you don't like it, tough luck! Even yet, it takes considerable time, money and planning to go anywhere else from there! This is why, with Australia, probably more than anywhere else, it is crucial to KNOW BEFORE YOU GO! – the sort of info that's in this book and not in many others.

....

Australia: aka Oz, the land down under, the land of the Southern Cross, the lucky country and the sunburnt country.

....

ABOUT THE AUTHOR

What are my credentials? In one word, <u>experience</u>. I am a detached observer who has learnt a great deal from lots of harsh first-hand experience over many years in many different countries. I've also had some of my poems published from time to time in anthologies, zines and websites like cynicalbastards.co.uk.

I come from that country where the states have really imaginative names like South Australia and Western Australia... where every suburb has a Crown Street, a Queen Street and a Victoria Road. What will they think of next? Don't ask who 'they' are. Aussies are not really supposed to ask questions. We're just supposed to consume, and be swept along by trends.

In Oz, the most common topics of conversation are usually sports, beer, the heat and the cockroaches. It is a nation which deludes itself (and the rest of the world) with spurious catch-phrases like 'the lucky country', 'fair go' etc. Try telling Aborigines that they've had a fair go in this country for the past two hundred years, and you'll soon get a different point of view.

In Australia, if you want to sell an idea or register a company name, it almost has to contain the words Oz, Aussie, Southern Cross or Down Under. And to be recognised in any form of print media, it almost has to contain the word icon or iconic. Such buzzwords have become so standard, that writers are hardly allowed to choose our own words any more. And it's all just empty hype about nothing in particular. It is a nation obsessed with itself and its own big ego; and also sold on British and American hoo-ha.

At least in my opinion, Oz has become a totally shallow, soulless dumbed-down, impersonal culture, if indeed it is worthy to be called a culture at all. Then there's 'multiculturalism' – a most convenient generic buzzword for the politicians to keep themselves covered with the front of political so-called correctness. In my opinion, 'multicultural' is a misnomer. Yes there are people in Australia from every other part of the world, and most of the time, they manage to tolerate each other; and so what? There is only *one* culture in Australia -- which they all have to adapt to – that is the culture of dumbed-down consumerism and standardisation gone mad.

I am an Aussie battler of sorts... not the tough outback kind, but nonetheless, i have had to battle in Australia like very few people do. I was born and raised in Sydney whether i liked it or not, and for the most part, i don't. Nobody really belongs in Sydney anymore. It just attracts pretentious people from everywhere else... people with a gold-rush mentality, who move there purely for economic reasons. Its most famous buildings are a bridge and an opera house, even though most Sydneysiders know more about Oprah than opera. In many such ways, Oz is ironic more than iconic.

A LAND OF IRONIC CONTRASTS. The Australia, the sun is brighter and more dangerous than anywhere else in the world. And keeping your eyes safe from its harmful rays is pretty much a full-time job. Nonetheless, Aussies are kept in the dark – a nation of mushrooms.

Aussies are not into creative bargaining or speculating.

If you think Britain is a nanny state, then you probably don't want to go to Australia!

If you are in Britain, the US or Canada, then don't go to Australia expecting any radical change of culture. It's much the same culture, just a different climate.

CULTURE AND MEDIA

In Australia, if you turn on almost any radio station or TV channel for five minutes, you'll soon notice it is a nation totally sold on mainstream dumbed-down commercial hype... like top 40 hottest hits, and the latest goss from Hollywood. And of course people there are spoilt for choice when it comes to sports coverage, since it's all a lot of Aussies give a damn about. The news is not really meant to inform. It's like: "a quick look at the bushfires... then sports and weather are next." Talk-back radio encourages no quality of debate worth talking about. So if you want anything truly informative or culturally specific, you'll have to lead a private life, with a well chosen inner circle of close friends, and your own collection of CDs and DVDs.

....

Did you know? In Australia,

- seven people commit suicide every day! (Those are just the ones who succeed, without counting the failed attempts).
- Sydney has a huge drug-problem: mainly ice or crystal meth.
- the national average IQ is not even 100: It's 95.

....

SEPARATING FACT
FROM FICTION

Have no illusions: Australia is a perennially hot, uncomfortable country to live in. If the unrelenting sun does not fatigue, burn or dehydrate you, then there's always the flies, the mozzies, snakes, spiders, sharks, crocs, stingers, blue-ringed octupi...what more do you want?...to test your endurance?

And when you're there, you are CONSTANTLY reminded that you are there. That is to say, especially in recent years, Oz has become obsessed with itself as much as America! There, all you ever hear about is Australian this, Aussie that, Aus this, Oz that etc. ... whether it's rock bands, beers, sports teams, insurance companies, whatever...almost as if no other country exists! – except of course, for one country they'll never be allowed to forget. Not everyone thinks it's "Great", so let's just call it Britain!

HOW BRITISH ARE THE AUSSIES? Apart from our larrikin attitude and our slangy twangy lingo, most Aussies are <u>almost as British as the British</u>. The paradox is: while Australia's weather and wild-life could hardly be more different from that of Britain, its government and institutions are boringly similar. So on one hand, many Aussies pride themselves on being from an apparently unique part of the world, yet, they're forever bound to be imitating the Brits somehow. Eg. The Queen's portrait is on the Aussie 5 dollar note: not on the 50, the 20 or the 10, but on the most common note which almost everyone has in their pocket at any one time. This is hardly accidental. So practically every time they put their hand in their pocket or open their wallet to pay for something, they're reminded that they are subjects of one of the richest women in the world, whether they do personally identify with her or not! It's not like Latin American countries, which long ago declared their independence from the Spanish Crown. The irony is, despite its <u>NATURAL</u> INDEPENDENCE as both an island and a continent, Australia will probably never be independent from the British. The republican movement has never really got off the ground. As vast as Australia is, it is also still a prison -- a land of no escape – from the sun, or the Crown.

As if it's not enough to have a Union Jack on the Aussie national flag, and 2 states (Queensland and Victoria) named after British queens, everywhere from Hobart to Darwin, virtually every major public place has names like Victoria Street, Queens' Park, Crown casino, The Theatre Royal and so on. What will the British think of next? Hence, Oz can be a very boring, monotonous country. And I'm not just talking about the way a lot of Aussies talk, or the lay of the land in the outback. While it's as big as Europe or the mainland US, it is not as diverse! <u>Australia's diversity is a popular lie</u> promoted by shallow travel-agents who've never been anywhere else! Unless:

-   you regard big rocks in the Red Centre as a vivid contrast to Sydney smog
-   or crocs in the north as a welcome sight after sharks or snakes. Take your pick!
-   you regard BrizVegas as a stark contrast to Star City Casino in Sydney or Crown casino in Melbourne.
-   one Aussie beer as radically different from another
-   you find one bottle of Cab Sav, Chardy or Shiraz delightfully different from the next

IS OZ REALLY FOR YOU?

This is a travel-guide with a twist. It is meant to be read BEFORE you go to Australia, to help you make up your mind if you want to go there or not. So, as much as anything, it tells you why <u>not</u> to go to Oz. Or it tests you to see –

-   how serious are you about wanting to go there?
-   Can you find what you want in other parts of the world?

If so, why go to Oz? Do ya really wanna go to this overrated desert wasteland which has got too big for its thongs?

Written by a rather contrarian Irish-Australian with a sense of ironic wit – who has travelled the continent extensively and gradually grown sick of it, it sheds new light on the brightest country in the world. Since everything's upside down in Oz, I thought I should write a non-travel-guide, an anti-travel guide, or a travel-guide away from Oz. A new genre of travel-writing?

It does not have glossy pics of Sydney Harbour, Bondi Beach, the Gold Coast, Uluru or kangaroos in the bush. You can find that stuff almost anywhere.

It also does not contain many trivial facts like "Cape Byron is the eastern-most point on the Australian mainland". So what?

Instead, this book tells you things most other travel-books won't: the less obvious stuff. It is for travellers who want to be better informed than the average tourist or backpacker.

GENERAL FACTS

As if the Aussie sun is not bright or hot enough, even during summer days, most public places there, such as cafes, pubs, train-stations, restaurants and so on...all have the lights (especially the super-bright spotlights) always on! – mainly for liability reasons. Especially in New South Wales, people are afraid of getting sued – even more than in most American states!

Basically, Oz is a society of insensitive, brain-washed bone-heads.

SHOULD I GO TO AUSTRALIA?

Make no mistake: Australia is <u>not</u> for everyone! And so it should not be attracting everyone from everywhere! And nowadays, it has serious issues as much as anywhere else, and population growth is one of them.

Many Asians assume that in Australia, over-crowding is not a problem, compared to what it's like in Asian cities. They should think again! Although Australia is a vast country, most of it is uninhabitable. Very few people want to live in the outback! So it has been a consensus for several decades that Australia cannot realistically support an ever-increasing population. Its population is now at around 23 million (June 2015) and rapidly increasing! Analysts are currently predicting that if the rate of population growth keeps increasing at the current rate, it's only a matter of time before the country has an environmental disaster! Australia now has a "minister for population". But no-one seems to know is that a minister for population growth or population control?I firmly believe that Australia's immigration controls should be as strict as its quarantine laws! Politically incorrect? So be it! The point?

DON'T COME TO AUSTRALIA UNLESS YOU'RE QUITE SURE THAT:

1. You can take the heat
2. You know what you're in for

3. You have an affinity for the <u>country</u>, not just for Sydney or BrisVegas.

Let's face it: Australia is sometimes called the arse end of the earth, or the arse-hole of the world, for pretty good reasons. So why go there?

- For sun and surf? You can find that off the coast of Brazil, Mexico, California, Florida, or the Med.
- Even if you share Steve Irwin's fetish for reptiles, you can get your arse bitten by crocs just as easily in parts of Africa, by snakes in South America, and by alligators in Louisiana and Florida.

A FALSE DEMOCRACY

Australia is a kind of false democracy. That is to say, it is a society in which people are brainwashed into thinking they have "choices" and a say in how it is run, when in reality they don't. Much like the weather – the "choice" is usually between hot and hotter. Likewise, with most other things, you can "choose" between sports and other sports, or between a range of similar beers. It's not really much of a choice.

In any truly democratic society, one size should <u>not</u> have to fit all, but in Australia, generally it does. While this is not said very often, it goes without saying. When it comes to choices, Oz is a great popular lie. By contrast, Europe is one continent with <u>many</u> countries, languages, cultures, styles of architecture and so on. Likewise with South America and Asia. But the hot hard fact about Australia is: it is one continent and only ONE country! So when you're there, if you find you don't like it, (for whatever reason/s), you have ONE very big problem! – as big as Australia itself!

In Oz, probably more than anywhere else, rightly or wrongly, ONE SIZE FITS ALL. And that doesn't apply just to insoles you buy in the chemist, or rain ponchos you buy from the discount store. It is a hard fact of life, right across the score-board!

"Mainstreaming" and "normalisation". These are buzzwords used by shallow counsellors and similar so-called professionals in relation to childrens' education. The consensus is that kids

who have special needs or learning difficulties should – as far as possible – be placed in mainstream public schools, not in "special" schools. I was an example of someone who was "mainstreamed" with disastrous consequences!

....

GENERAL TRENDS

Now more than ever, Oz has become a culture of dumbed down consumerism and standardisation gone mad... a nation obsessed with its own economic growth, and hooked on pop culture and all things virtual instead of real... with everyone leading their own selfish little lives, with little if any sense of community or belonging to anything except a nanny welfare state.

This country has all but wiped out any indigenous shamanism or spirituality it ever had! ... in the name of hypocritical buzzwords like a "fair go", "progress", "multi-culturalism" and "Judeo-Christian values." I mean, even an intelligent high-school kid should be able to see through it, but most Australian adults are not supposed to. We're just supposed to be pot-bellied gluttonous sports-mad consumers, content with the bright sun, glass-half-full thinking and dumbed-down snippets of so-called news on the tv and radio.... fooling ourselves into thinking that the rest of the world has all gone to Hell, and that Oz is the only place to live.

If you want to observe these trends in action, there is no better place than a shopping mall, especially the food court or eatery. It is a gluttons' paradise! with outlets selling almost every imaginable kind of food and drink under one big roof, in throw-away plastic containers and take-away paper cups, which all go in the bins. Most are not recyclable. And most shoppers wouldn't think of taking them home, washing them and re-using them. Meanwhile, we're bombarded by in-your-face advertising on billboards, on the net, on tv and radio – telling us what we've got to want, to love, the next must-have offer from McDonald's, Vodafone or whoever. Next-door neighbours tell each other things like "You've gotta

get a TV mate! Else you're out of touch. You'll go crazy without one."
"I can get ya a good deal on a set-top box and a dvd; hook it up and
she'll be right." This is about as hospitable as Aussies get. If they ever
do get to know their neighbours, it's purely in terms of such flippant
assumptions and material values.

> Our quality of life is all just economics:
> while our sense of being 'connected' is all just electronics.

What about the fact that people also have **emotional** needs, **spiritual**
needs and the like? A need to belong somewhere, not just to be one more
pension number or one more consumer or statistic. In such soulless
societies, such natural human needs are hardly ever even acknowledged,
much less met!

Australia has now become a total nanny state and a police state.

It has a long history of government schemes and false or empty promises.

Oz is overwhelmingly a country for sports-mad hedonists, with a beer in
one hand, a mobile in the other, ear-phones in their ear, fishing tackle in
their ute or 4x4 -- and a love of the great outdoors. If you're not that way
inclined, there is not much place for you there…unless you're content to
smoke and drink yourself to death among a few marginalised libertines
in Melbourne's underground arts scene.

....

WEATHER

If there's one thing most people can agree on, it's usually the weather. And in Oz, you hardly need the forecast to tell you that it's usually gunna be too bloody hot! Almost any day of the year is bound to turn out hotter than expected.

Aborigines have always realised that Australia does not actually have four seasons, like most other countries. Nonetheless, the British settlers and Europeans insist on thinking of it in terms of their four seasons reversed. Get this, the "Autumn" is often even hotter than the "summer". But there is usually not much seasonal variety. Not many autumn leaves or spring flowers – or not for long. So, to make it simpler, there's usually only <u>two</u> seasons: bearably hot, and <u>un</u>bearably freakin' <u>hot!!</u>

Australia is often called "the Lucky Country", even though, most days, you can count yourself "lucky" if you can "beat the heat" and avoid getting sun-burnt or stung by something. Never mind ambition, social-life or anything else.

THE AUSSIE SUN

When the BritIsh tried to ensure that the sun would never set on their soulless empire, they made a very shrewd choice by colonising Australia. In Oz, there is rarely if ever any escape from that burning, blinding sun! In almost any part of the continent, at almost any time of year, most afternoons, it indeed seems like it's never going to set!

Especially if you have pale skin, <u>take no chances with the sun</u>! If you do, you can get severely sun-burned faster than ockers can say "Let's-get-on-the-*piss*-mate". That's quick! This is especially true from about 11 am to around 4 pm on most days. During that time, wear sun-screen lotion, especially round ya neck, shoulders and nose. It's better to rub it in, so it's not obvious. Especially if you're going in the water, you should re-apply the lotion a couple of times a day – once every few hours.

Don't assume you won't need your umbrella or scarf in Oz. They can come in handy – for protecting you from the sun!

The danger of the sun is mainly due to the whole in the ozone layer, which is above Australia. This is because for decades, Aussies have been – per capita – the worst polluters on the planet. And even yet, Victoria's environmental record lags well behind the rest of Australia.

If there are two parts of Oz where you can sometimes escape the sun and its heat, they are Melbourne and Tasmania in the winter.

WAYS TO BEAT THE HEAT

Wherever possible, walk on the shady side of the street, not the sunny side! That's where thinking negative is positive.

Wear light-coloured clothes, not dark, so they'll reflect the sun off ya.

If you're a woman with a baby in a pram or stroller, drape a white or similarly light-coloured sheet, towel or something like that over the pram or stroller, to keep your child sheltered from the sun. Don't use a black or dark blue one! That will attract and absorb the sun, and make your baby feel even hotter!

Keep a damp scarf in your fridge or freezer. Wear it round your neck when you go out. It stops your neck from getting sun-burnt, and reduces your overall body temperature.

Use a light-coloured umbrella to keep the sun off ya.

If possible, or if you have a choice, stay in rooms on the ground floor or in basements – where it's cooler; not on the top floor – where it's hottest.

Go for a swim in an indoor pool.

Go somewhere where they've got air-con: like a cinema, library, or major shoppin'-cenna.

WINTER

Yep, some parts of Oz do have a "winna." You'll feel the cold there, because most of the houses are not well insulated against it. They're full of cracks and holes... they're not built solidly like they are in Europe. And if you think you won't catch a cold or flu there, think again! Even then, most Aussies still wear shorts and thongs, and drink booze, so they usually do catch a cold or flu. Furthermore, with their casual lack of manners, they usually don't cover their mouths when they cough or sneeze. So in winter, germs spread as fast as bush-fires in summer!

ACCOMMODATION
(more commonly called accom)

BOARDING HOUSES

Unless you're "off ya tree" or a tough Aussie battla, they're generally not to be recommended. They're usually the cheapest option, but...

whether licensed or not, they tend to attract skanky sorts of women and thuggish sorts of guys.

So you do pay hidden prices. If a place is "a boarding house", that's a magic excuse to justify practically any kind of mismanagement or neglect. They tend to harbour deranged sorts, like druggies, jailies and mental cases.

Keep your expectations low!
Don't expect meals or bed linen to be included in the rent. (LOL!)
Watch ya back as well as ya gear.

BACKPACKER HOSTELS. If there's one or two words which can be taken literally in dumbed-down Aussie English, then they are backpack and backpacking. In other words, if you don't have a full-sized backpack on you, many hostels will not allow you in. Do they want to make sure your travels will be as burdensome as possible? I gave up trying to understand backpacker logic yonks ago. But i think i can safely say the following. As in most countries, hostels tend to be of two kinds:

- the ultra-clinical, sterile dehumanised YHA variety, or
- the opposite extreme: flea-pits full of bed-bugs, run by time-wasting pot-smoking jerks who justify any kind of mismanagement in the magic name of "laid back" or "chilled out atmosphere".

Take your pick. Either way, thieves thrive in them. If ya wanna know how inhospitable a culture can be, they're a good place to start.

HOTELS -- SEE PUBS

HOUSES. By the way…practically every house in Oz has spiders, cockroaches and termites. And you'll feel the cold in winna, cuz they're full o' cracks and holes… they're not built solid or well insulated like they are in Europe.

....

AUSTRALIANA / SOUVENIRS

PROUDLY AUSTRALAIN OWNED -- MADE IN CHINA

If you go into most souvenir shops in the cities, you'll soon notice most of them are staffed by Chinese people. Yes, they're just as dinky-di Aussie as anyone – since the gold-rush in the 1800s, yes absolutely. But don't expect them to spin you a yarn about the so-called Australiana you're purchasing…its history or authenticity. No no! They'll just say something like "Ten dollar fifty. Next?' Is their reticence just because their English no very good? Or are they hiding something? Well, when you read the fine print on the label, it will usually say "MADE IN CHINA". It's all a bit of a farce, and they know it.

If most Aussie convicts could come out of their cells and be straight about one thing, it would probably be that most goods which are "made in Australia" are not even worth shoplifting! We can't blame the Chinese for that. Apart from that, nearly everything else is defective junk made in China, which is bound to last about as long as the milk in the fridge. Take your pick! /

If Aussie convicts ever come out of their cells and talk straight about one thing, they'll have to admit that **neither goods made in Australia or in China are even worth shoplifting!**

EATING AND DRINKING

Relevant strine: tucker = food in general. Tuck in! = Go ahead, enjoy your meal.

ONE PRICE FITS ALL. If you hail from a Latin or South-east Asian culture, you're in for at least two shocks in Oz.

1. Australians are not hospitable personable people.
2. They've are into creative bargaining.

Eg. If you to eat out, for take-away food, be it a burger, kebab or whatever, suppose you want it without the chilli, the onions and the mushrooms, the price still remains the same. If you don't want those things, why should you have to pay for them? If you ask this to your average meat-head behind a counter, you'll probably get an answer like "Dunno....that's just the way it is." So if you have food allergies or intolerances, then fact is, you do have to pay for the stuff you can't eat or don't want!

A NATIONAL DISH? Unless you wanna eat witchiti-grubs in a vegemite damper roll, Australia doesn't have much in the way of home-grown culinary tradition. Hence probably the closest thing Oz has to a national dish is – believe it or not – "Spag Bol". (Most Aussies are too lazy to say "Spaghetti Bolognese" or Bolognaise). So Spag Bol it is.

In the supermarkets, when even the cheapest home brand olive oil is called "Extra Virgin", it makes you wonder, are we all being screwed?!

Then there's about 100 different sorts of yoghurts, but they're all touted as 95 or 99% fat free! So it's a choice that's not really a choice. If that's not a big enough insult to your intelligence, when you look for the INGREDIENTS on the label, it often says simply "Made from the finest quality ingredients" or "Made in Australia from local and imported ingredients", or "No artificial colours, flavours or preservatives'. That still doesn't tell you what is actually in it. Then many of them have cute French names like Fruche, Yoplait and fromage frais, even though in French, fromage is cheese, not yoghurt. Fact is, most Aussies don't really know what they're feeding themselves and their kids (apart from bullshit). No wonder so many of them just acquire a taste for a certain beer and stick to it.

BEER

Let's face it: It's all a lot of Aussies have got in them, apart from sports-scores. So ya midas well get ta like it. Fosters is mostly an export beer. So in Oz, you usually won't find it in pubs. If you see it advertised, chances are, it's just an outdated sign – like memorabilia, not current info. Castlemaine XXXX is pronounced simply as "four ex". (Aussies wouldn't be bothered to say ex-ex-ex-ex or double-ex double-ex).

WINE AND CHEESE

If you come from countries like France, Switzerland or Italy – which have mature notions about wines and cheeses and how they should taste – then keep your expectations low when it comes to sampling such things in Oz. <u>In short, they're shit!</u> But if you come from the States, where most cheese is that orange, hyperplastic gum you put in cheese-burgers, then okay, you might find Aussie cheese to be a welcome relief, or a less toxic rubber substitute.

"Award-winning" wines? Don't be impressed by people who talk shallow wine talk, to try to persuade you to come on some pricey wine tour of the Hunter or Barossa Valley. Almost every wine in Australia wins some award at some time or another. So when you see a bottle of

Shiraz or Merlot with 6 or 8 little gold, silver or bronze medal stickers stuck along the edge of the label, no, it's usually <u>not</u> worth the extra cash. And unless you're a connoisseur, there is little if any discernible difference in quality between a ten buck bottle o' plonk, and one you pay $89.99 for.

And most wines which are advertised as "full-bodied" are usually so watery, you might as well water the plants with them.

"Cask wine" is a euphemism for cheap nasty piss in silver foil bags in cardboard boxes. Even backpackers can do better than that.

It's all a bit of a rort.

Don't buy wine by the glass in pubs …their so-called 'house red' or 'house white'. They charge you around 6 bucks for this half glass of vile-tasting piss. And in a society of glass-half-full thinking, you can't complain. How convenient!

PUBS

Whether you're a pub sort of person or not, there are a couple of open secrets that are worth knowing about pubs in Oz.

1. Though they're officially called hotels, most of them rarely actually have any accommodation.
2. Basically, <u>they're geared for fuckwits</u>! Most of their revenue comes from Poker-machines (more often called pokies or pokes). Most pubs also have a range of similar fools' games like raffles, jackpots, Joker Poker, trivia contests and the like – where, in effect, you throw your cash down the drain to win a chance to win a chance to win a prize – occasionally cash, but more often, football caps, eskies or meat trays. Assuming you're not a fuckwit, don't fall for them.

Sad but true: Aussie pubs have become very impersonal. Many of them don't even have bar-stools round the bar any more! So at least in the cities, the days of groups of people sitting round the bar, spinning yarns, telling jokes or chatting up the bar-maids are history! And even if you frequent the same pub for twenny years, don't expect any sense of customer loyalty or any such rapport. To them, you'll always be just another few bucks in the till. Next?

Especially if you come from Latin or Mediterranean countries – where hospitality is a human quality – you're in for a shock in Oz. Australian "hospitality" is just an *industry* like any other. Its first and final concern is money, and going along with trends and standards.

If you look like you've already had a drink or two, they can refuse to serve you. But this still doesn't stop drunken hoons from going out in their hot-rod sports-cars and getting killed in accidents. So at least in my opinion, the alcohol restrictions are in the wrong places, or not well implemented.

"How many drinks have you had?" This is the most common question most bouncers ask customers who walk a bit wobbly or who act a bit boozy. I don't think it's a good way to test someone's sobriety. When someone is half-pissed, they can easily come up with smart-arsed answers like "As many as i want", or "Only one... a whole big bottle o' Bundy."

LEMON LIME & BITTERS is quite a good non-alcoholic substitute for beer, and it's cheaper. And as long as it tastes sweet enough, no-one seems to know or care what bitters actually are. On the label of the bottle, it just says they're 1%. Aussies are not meant to be well informed.

SOCIAL LIFE

SOCIAL ATTITUDES / FITTING IN / SOCIAL LIFE

Even in the cities, socially and culturally, Australia can be just as dry as the outback. In order to tolerate living in Australia, it would help tremendously if you've got no brains and you're happy without them. That makes you a so-called "positive" person.

There is a subtle kind of political so-called 'correctness' – a popular lie of so-called "multi-culturalism", which means simply that in the big cities, yes, there are lots of people from most other countries. But so what? When you meet them, especially Asians, generally they don't like to be asked where they're from. If you ask them where they're from, they usually say 'Bondi', "Fitzroy" or whatever suburb they live in. They seem to be afraid of being discriminated against. If Australia was truly multi-cultural or politically correct, then they wouldn't have to have that fear! Would they? And if we Aussies are not even supposed to ask where they're from, then how can we get to know them? -- if they don't want to talk about their country, culture or heritage? Hence, Oz is a very divided society. There are the Aborigines, the white Australians, and the "New Australians" (the Chinese, Muslims etc) – who live more or less as separate groups in different suburbs. Mind you, increasingly, you do see Asians in pubs, acquiring a taste for beer, but surprise surprise, they usually sit in groups of other Asians -- yapping to each other in their own language. The more things change, the more they stay the same.

Migrants expect to be accepted as "Australians" as soon as possible. But to this end, it would help if they:

- learnt a few things about Australia before they arrived,
- learnt some English, apart from just the word "dollar",
- and tried to integrate more, instead of just spending their whole lives selling junk-food in corner-shops.

The other point of view is however, it is hard for them to integrate, because they know a lot of Aussies are still racist. Besides, it's never gunna matter to them (the migrants) who Donald Bradman was, or who wrote Waltzing Matilda – (and all that sort of traditional Aussie knowledge). As long as they can make a buck, why should they give a fuck?

If some of them are of an interesting ethnic mix – eg. If someone is a Filipino who is somehow also part Irish and part Jewish, then why don't they make it a talking-point? Surely that would help to break the ice with a lot of people – instead of keeping it as some kind of shameful secret. Anyway, that's what political "correctness" does to people -- at least in Australia.

The "Asian invasion" is arguably the best thing that's happened to Australia in over two hundred years. Asians tend to be better brought up than Aussies, and more hard-working, while Aussies are lazy. Oz has been run by racist convicts for long enough.

Many people have the idea that since most Aussies seem so casual and easy-goin', that Australia has little if any social pressures. Expressions like "She'll be right mate" and "No worries" seem to perpetuate this humourous post-card image of Oz -- as a place that's still quite safe and far-removed from the stresses of the rest of the world. Although this book employs that sort of humour as well, it's an outdated perception.

Fact is, every society has some sort of pressure to conform to something, and Australia is no exception. What it lacks in terms of social formalities, it makes up for in terms of strict laws and hefty fines and taxes regarding quarantine, alcohol consumption, speeding on the roads, and many other restrictions too numerous to mention here. So as with anywhere, the safest principle to follow is "When in Oz, do as the Ozzies do". That is to say:

1. Drink beer, call it 'piss', but <u>don't drink and drive above .05!</u>
2. At least in summer, wear thongs, even though they're bad for your feet in the long term.
3. Adopt totally materialistic, popular, crap-head values. Want (or at least pretend to want) ipods, wireless broadband, a big plasma TV or three, the latest play-station, double garage, back-yard pool, 4WD, GPS, whatever the latest gimmick is… yep…the whole kit n' koala.
4. At least try to fake some interest in some sort of sports or outdoor activities.
5. Try and keep your conversation and opinions dumbed-down -- to appeal to the lowest common denominator. (It's not France or Germany in terms of intellectual life).
6. At least in pubs, try to avoid conversations about politics, philosophy, or anything heady or controversial. (If you've got mature thoughts or opinions about issues or anything other than sports or beer, you might be told to keep them quiet, or take them somewhere else.). Instead, just talk glass-half-full shit 'til ya gut's full o' piss... and you'll be right.
7. As if the fire-danger's not high enough in summer in any case, get the barbie out, stoke it up, chuck a few snags or shrimps on it, and smoke everyone out of the back yard. What a rippa! Just kidding.

REAL AUSTRALIANS?

Arguably, the only fair dink Aussies are the Aborigines, but they're only about 1 or 2 per cent of the population, and in Tasmania, they've died out completely! And most of them prefer to call themselves "indigenous" instead of "Australian".

Meanwhile, almost anyone from anywhere can call themselves "new Australians", even if they know less about Australia than you've already learnt from this book. So, <u>who are the real Australians??</u> It's a difficult sociological question. To try to answer it seriously would go beyond the scope of this book. But at least in my view, the real Australians are <u>the people who've paid the price</u> of living in Oz! – whether they liked it or not. Eg. People who've lost their homes in bush-fires, farmers who have to battle long droughts and so on. The convicts were not the only people who've been "imprisoned" in Oz. And the early settlers were not the only people to have a very hard time here, and they won't be the last. I think it's fair to say that they are the real Australians.

However, any notion of being "true blue", fair dinkum or dinky di Aussie has become harder and harder to defend in recent decades. In many people's eyes, it has little if any credibility. Instead, it has laughability along the lines of Kevin Bloody Wilson, Col Elliott, Rodney Rude and let's not forget Paul Hogan (better known to the rest of the world as Crocodile Dundee).

If there still is anything worth defending as fair dinkum Aussie, you won't find it in cities like Sydney or Melbourne, also often called "the big smoke."

MATESHIP

Let's burst this bubble of bull for once and for all! Aussie mateship is shallow friendship which can be summed up as "easy come, easy go, mate." It usually depends on which beer you drink, which footy-team you barrack for, or what sort of ute you drive. It is no guarantee of long-term trust, and Americans get over it – it's not about mating in any sexual sense of the word... except maybe in Newtown or Darlinghurst (the two most gay suburbs of Sydney).

ROMANCE

Australians are not romantic people. They have to look to cheesy British and American films to get some idea what romance might be. Any notion they ever had of romance pretty much died in the arse with Aussie blokes asking women things like "G'day Sheila – ja wanna fuck?" If that's not a formula for failure, then nowadays, blokes can also get easily "done" for sexual harassment. Furthermore, surveys have shown the thing which most Aussie women find the most unattractive in men is a beer-gut; and surprise surprise, that's what most Aussie blokes have got.

DIVERSITY/ VARIETY? In Oz, every "occasion" is just another excuse to get on the piss with ya mates: New Year's, Australia Day (Jan 26 or 27), Easter, Christmas, birthday parties – you name it. So there's no real sense of occasion about anything. Hence, most blokes have got more ties than they'll ever have occasion to wear. And in op shops, you can find heaps of ties for about a buck each.

Where's the variety in a society where every "variety store" is the same?

....

STATE BY STATE

The following is not meant to be a comprehensive travel guide – just a quick overview of some parts of Oz.

SYDNEY It is the state capital of New South Wales, but not the national capital. It is one of the most gay cities in the world with a huge ice habit. Beyond that, it changes so fast, there's not much point in writing about it.

CANBERRA is the national capital – a totally sterile soulless city that was planned all at the same time. Once a year it hosts a hot air balloon festival. How symbolic! Just in case there ever was any doubt, the pollies are full of hot air!

MELBOURNE used to be the nation's capital, and as such, its streets have been named after the Brits even more than Sydney. Apart from Athens, it has the biggest Greek population of any city in the world. It has an extensive network of trams, which makes it arguably a more efficient better organised city than Syd. Plus musicians, artists and writers have always preferred Melbourne to Syd. It has a different sort of poetry scene. But of course beach bums prefer Sydney, since Sydney has around twenty beaches, where Melbourne has one or two, with more English weather.

BRISBANE AKA BRIZVEGAS – It's similar to London and Melbourne. The name says it all.

BYRON BAY - often simply called "Byron". The eastern-most point on the mainland. It has an excellent weekend market where you can sample a brilliant range of exotic foods and drinks. Byron's popularity has no doubt been boosted by the fact that Paul Hogan and Linda Koslowski? used to live in a huge house there. But mainly, it's just where surfers and backpackers go to get wasted.

THE NORTHERN TERRITORY – AKA THE TOP END

Even if you've got a skin as thick as a croc
and a Darwin thirst for beer,
think twice before you head out
for Australia's last frontier.

TASMANIA aka "Down under down under" and the "Apple Isle", because it is roughly the shape of an apple, and they grow good apples there.

It's the most expensive part of Australia. Being an island, most goods have to be imported there from the mainland. And apart from freight-trains, it has no trains. Cars or coaches only. It's a good state to go to to retire or to die, but not to get a life. It's got good fresh seafood and raspberry soda, but apart from wild wilderness and devils, Tasmanians don't seem to have much else to talk about.

Tassie (pronounced Tazzy) is still quite isolated: hard to get to from the mainland, and hard to get out of once you're there. Apart from the Sydney to Hobart yaucht race, there isn't actually any boat or ship service that goes from Sydney to Hobart or vice versa. Instead, there's a boat called the Spirit of Tasmania that goes from Melbourne to Devonport and vice versa. It takes about nine hours to cross Bass Strait.

HOBART is like Sydney on a smaller scale: a harbour, with old convict architecture around it, a big bridge, a casino (Wrest Point), even a shopping centre in the middle called Centrepoint, and a big chess-set in the park, a bit smaller than the one in Hyde Park or St James Park in Sydney. And if that doesn't make them a crowd of soulless imitators, there's also a red double-decker tour-bus, just like the ones in Sydney and London.

Hobart is the closest thing Taz has to a vibrant city. But even there, opening hours of pubs, businesses and all that are boringly restricted.

Salamanca market is certainly worth visiting. In that area there's a pub called "Irish Murphy's", as if the name "Murphy's" wouldn't sound Irish enough by itself.

NATURAL WONDERS.

> The Great Barrier Reaf is endangered.
> the Blue mountains, Kakadu National park

THE RED CENTRE

Many people go to Alice springs, Uluru and Kata tjuta national park, more or less in the same trip.

ALICE SPRINGS – aka Alice or the Alice. Has around thirty thousand people. It's a long way from the beach.

Uluru. It's better to call it Uluru (its proper Aboriginal name) instead of Ayer's Rock. It has been sacred to indigenous peoples for tens of thousands of years. They don't like people climbing on it or standing on the top of it.

WESTERN AUSTRALIA – more often simply called WA. Kalgoorlie is a very hot mining town. Kev Wilson wrote some interesting love songs about it.

The Nullarbor plain has no trees.

....

ESOTERIC BELIEFS

Oz does not strike most people as a deeply mystical place. And indeed, most white Australians are about as spiritual or mystical as sportsbet. com.au. In Oz, so-called spiritual or psychic healing, astrology, palmistry, etc, is almost entirely a commercialised rip-off business, (much the same as in the UK), which will cost you on average – at least 2 bucks a minute, in new age shops full of incense and other things you'll be persuaded to buy. Any genuine shamans, soothsayers or sages Australia might have are likely to be Aboriginal or Torres Strait Islanders. But they are very few and far between. And you won't find them working in rip-off shops in Sydney.

LUCKY NUMBERS? Whether or not you are a believer in such things, it might be worth knowing – before you go -- that when it comes to superstitions and numerology, Australia seems to be sub-consciously addicted to the Devil, and bad luck in general! Either that, or, it regards the whole thing as a joke. At least in Sydney, the number 13 is practically inescapable! Likewise with "the Devil's number" 666. It is often used as the last few digits of the phone-numbers of brothels. Most phone numbers start with 13. It's common for taxi companies for instance, to have phone numbers like 13 13 33. So don't expect them to arrive on time.

In late Jan. 2010, in Dulwich Hill, in Sydney's inner west, one day I was walking down a street, and outside a newsagent, there was a Lotto ad, advertising a cash prize up for grabs of $ 666,666.67! If that's the worst "devil" Aussies ever have to deal with, they can count themselves lucky indeed.

There are permanent signs and flags outside many barber shops saying things like "Haircut $13". Why not $10 or 15? Out of all possible numbers, why 13? These are questions most Aussies are not supposed to ask, and not supposed to answer.

If you're a believer in the power of words, names or sounds, you can often tell a lot about a country by its name; especially by the sound of the stressed syllable. Eg. The way most Italians say *"Italia"* does sound quite italicised. The way a lot of the Irish say "Ireland" does sound full of ire – an old word for anger. And the way a lot of Aussies say "Australia" sounds more like "Stray-a" -- a distant place where you go astray? Backpacking for a few years to try and find yourself? The way they say "Australian" often sounds like "Strayin'". Mmmm....there seems to be a definite pattern.

TECHNOLOGY AND TRANSPORT

Australia has become <u>obsessed</u> with technology – so much so that if our shallow culture hasn't made us stupid, so much exposure to sat-nav probably will.

Yet, in terms of fast, efficient transport and communications, Oz lags a long way behind truly advanced societies like France, Germany and Japan.

Sydney buses are often frustratingly slow, compared to the pace of the rest of the traffic. At every stop, drivers have to fumble around for ten minutes – giving change to most people who get on...until everyone is eventually packed in like sardines. So then at the next stop, how is anyone supposed to get off??. The drivers let too many passengers on the bus.... even on the "no standing" areas of the floor. They have shit for brains! And if you complain to most drivers, their typical "solution" is that *you* should get off the bus and catch another one. That's not the point, and it's not a solution. But it's a quick fix for them. Sydney buses contain about 20 red circle signs saying "no smoking", no alcohol, no feet on the seats, no this, no that…but there's no-one who can enforce them. False rules, false promises, false friends – all just "swings and roundabouts" as they say.

FROM PENAL SETTLEMENT TO PRISON

Australia has more laws, rules and restrictions than anyone can ever enforce, first and foremost quarantine laws. Don't bring any organic matter into Oz, like food or plants from anywhere else. And if you wouldn't try to smuggle drugs through Singapore or Kuala Lumpur, then don't try it in Oz either.

COMMUNICTIONS
AND LANGUAGE

INTERNET CAFES. At least in Sydney, public internet access is becoming very limited. Internet cafes go out of business all the time, probably because most people have their own laptops.

PUBLIC PHONES are also becoming practically a thing of the past, probably because of mobile phones.

ASKING DIRECTIONS. At least in Sydney, almost everyone's got an ipod stuck in their ear. So if you get lost, asking a fellow human being for directions in the street is virtually a privilege of the past.

Apart from "G'day", the most common ice-breaker is "It's a bloody hot one today!' – with a tone of ominous resignation.

The most common topics of conversation are usually sports, beers, the heat and the cockroaches.

If ya wanna learn to talk like a dumbed-down Aussie boofhead, then this book will tell ya how… so much so that after reading this, ya mates will think you've spent about ten years down under, even if you haven't been there at all!

If ya wanna be a sports-mad consumer in a throw-away society, then Oz is probably the best country in the world.

Aussie pubs are geared totally for beer-bellied boofheads, punters and the like.

STRINE. Strine is Aussie slang. It's like, when lazy bushies say the word "Australian", it usually sounds more like Strayin' or Strine. These days in the major cities, strine is pretty much a thing of the past. It's more a regional thing among older folks.

....

A TYPICAL AUSSEI CONVERSATION

Person 1. It's gunna be a hot one today! (in a tone of ominous resignation)
Person 2. Aw yeah... and even hodda t'morra they reckon.
P1. An' even hodda erry day fr'at least a week!
P2. Bloody oath!
P1: Anyway, see ya.

The magic little word go

Aussies use the word go in probably more subtly different ways than any other people. Here's a rundown of the most common slang ways.

"Wot's the go 'ere?" In this case, the go is the deal, or the general rule of thumb, be it self-service, BYO, all-u-can-eat, wait to be seated, or whatever. Wot was the go this mornin'?' = What were u so annoyed about this morning?" or what was that all about?'

"Go on, have a go!" This is quite a festive way to encourage someone to participate in a fun game or sporting event. However, to go can also mean to fight. "Aw yeah? Ya wanna *go*?" = "Ya wanna start a **blue** about it.' It is a subtle difference in context.

(of a person, dog or horse) To run fast. "Look at 'im go!"

Go can also be a noun, meaning motivation in general. "If the Sheilas have got a bit of *go* about them, they get'em drivin' the semis."

....

ABBREVIATIONS AND ACRONYMS

In Oz, the number of abbreviations and acronyms is practically endless. Eg re wines:

Cab sav = Cabernet Sauvignon.   Ssb = semillion sauvignon blanc.

ACRONYMS

If Aussies have one linguistic skill, (apart from talking through the side of their mouths to keep the flies out), it is that of abbreviation, which they take to extremes. So Australia is one country where it certainly does pay to know your abbreviations and acronyms – especially three-letter ones. Not surprisingly, most of them start with A.

> AAA – Australian Automobile Association
> ABC – Australian Broadcasting Corp
> AHA – Australian Hotels Association
> AMA – Australian Medical Association
> ACCC – Aust Competition and Consumer Commission
> AEST – Aust Eastern Standard Time (Sydney time)
> ASIC – Aust Securities and Investment Commission
> ASIO – Aust Security and Intelligence Org
> ASX = Australian Securities Exchange
> ATO – Aust Taxation Office

Google the rest if ya wanna.

This is true nowadays more than ever since PM Kevin Rudd who coined a few of his own. He called the global financial crisis the GFC, his Deputy Prime Minister (Julia Gillard) the DPM, and early childhood education – yep, you guessed it -- ECE. And he called the Gonski reforms simply "better schools." How's *that* for dumbing down? I mean anyone who's ever finished school should know that "better" is a relative term which begs the question -- better than what?

But how is anyone supposed to know or remember if ALP stands for Australian Labor Party or Australian Liberal Party? And why do they spell Labor the American way – omitting the u? These are things most Aussies are not really supposed to know.

But even the most drunk sports fan knows a lot about the AFL (Aust Football League), the NRL (National Rugby League), the SCG (Sydney Cricket Ground), the MCG (Melbourne Cricket Ground), and probably more others than any book could ever include.

If you're into classical music, there's the ACO (Aust Chamber Orchestra), the SSO (Sydney Symphony Orchestra) and the MSO (Melbourne Symphony Orchestra).

And of course no matter what you're into, the government gets the GST (Goods and Services Tax) out of you, on virtually everything every day.

Then most of the states and territories have acronyms too. Folks from Western Australia more readily refer to it as WA. The rest are just as easy:

ACT = Aust Capital Territory	SA = South Australia
NSW= New South Wales	QLD = Queensland
NT = Northern Territory	TAS / Tassie (pronounced
VIC = Victoria, and last but not least,	Tazzy) = Tasmania

Aussies have a very short way with words. They mince words, and sometimes even let certain words go without sayin' at all. Eg. Local [pub], domestic [row or fight], email [address], mobile [phone] and so on.

Reggo = [vehicle] registration. Cuppa [tea]

CONVERSATION?

There is a strange, underlying fact about Australian English, which very few Australians and even fewer books will ever admit: that is: **Most Aussies don't actually converse!** They talk cliché fragments or snippets. In a pub or shop, a typical Aussie 'conversation' (between cashier and customer) goes something like this:

G'day..........................How's it goin'?.........Orrright.
It's a hot one today...........Bloody oath!
Watchin' the footy?.........For sure.
Five bucks fifty...............Tah. / Rightio / She'll be right / Cheers.
No worries.....................See ya...... On ya.

But hang on; **who**'s saying **what** here? Isn't a dialogue supposed to indicate that? Is this supposed to read across in rows, or down in columns? Well that's the strangely clever thing about it. Most of these common cornerstones of Aussie English are virtually interchangeable. So they can be read either way, or said by either person in almost any order. So there's hardly any train of thought required! Intellectual curiosity is certainly not encouraged. Reason and speculation are tolerated if and only if they contain calculations about likely outcomes of sporting-events, or large amounts of money blown on pokies or piss.

Glass-half-full goss is the norm. If you have a mind of your own – that is to say -- opinions, judgments, persuasions, tastes or insights which are in any way uncommon, then you must learn not to express them. If you do, you'll simply be branded as 'negative', told to stop 'complaining', or frankly told to pipe down, shut up, "pull ya head in" or go somewhere else.

If you value intellectual rapport, well-informed debate, TV shows which are usually worth watching, or rich or spicy foods, then Oz is probably **not** the country for you.

Let's face it: most Aussies are essentially dumbed-down poms. So they should be forgiven for being – let's say – not the most well-cultured culture. In fact it could well be argued that Australia is hardly a culture at all!…at least not in any strict sense. As in Oz, things like family values, social hierarchies, religions, spiritual beliefs and the like…have virtually no influence worth talking about.

If something doesn't make a buck, it's usually not talked about…or not for long.

And last but not least, a lot of Aussie blokes call each other "cunts" (Sorry ladies), simply cuz that is wot a lot of 'em are.

AUSLAN or auslan is Australian sign language for the hearing-impaired. If you have to converse with deaf people in Oz, at least learn the hand-gestures for beer, sports, and "Good on ya". They swear in sing-language too.

NRS – the National Relay Service is a phone system for people who are hearing impaired or who have a speech impediment.

> www.relayservice.gov.au/contact/helpdesk
> helpdesk@relayservice.com.au
> 1800 555 660 (1800 numbers are toll free from landlines)
> TTY 1800 555 630   TTY is also called a teletypewriter textphone.

PUBLIC SERVICES

In Oz as in most countries, depending on public services is usually the surest way to get nowhere, except round and around the runaround, while "government initiative" is a contradiction in terms. Everyone knows the gov's got no initiative, except when it comes to raising revenue.

TRANSPORT

Australia is not really an advanced nation in this regard. Sydney buses tend to be frustratingly slow compared to the pace of Sydney traffic and life in general. With good air-con and upholstery, they are a luxury for people who have time to waste, like retirees, crips, and people who are so obese they can't fit into small modern cars.

Meanwhile, Sydney trains generally chug along about as fast as a fit person could jog. The XPT (the fastest intercity trains) are not much faster. Small wonder that at many regional tourist info centres, there is sometimes an ad showing a train heading out over a vast outback plain….and the slogan says "Australia – a land you'll never get over". Well of course you'll never get over it, at 30 km an hour!

Melbourne is arguably a more efficient, better organised city.

In Tas, there are no public trains: only freight trains.

TRAINS are also for people who have plenty of time to spend taking the scenic route – millions of kilometers of gumtrees and shrub.... or countless towns and cities which all look the same, thanks to standardisation-gone-mad. Is that really getting somewhere? Why not just go to a different country right from the start?

LIBRARIES

Public libraries in Oz are hardly places of assiduous study. They are very "kid-friendly" and "open to everyone". In fact this means they are effectively playgrounds for kids to run riot and borrow a stack of DVDs on the way out.

....

Australia has now become a total nanny state and a police state.

It has a long history of government schemes, false hopes and empty promises.

SPORTS

Sport is so much a part of the way Aussies relate to each other, that it cannot be underestimated or understated!

If Aussies ever have well-informed opinions or discerning observations about anything apart from beer, they're usually about sports.

So they can soon tell if you don't follow any sport in particular. Then unless you're rich or famous, they lose interest in you very fast. It's orright to tell'em if you don't follow golf, Origin, AFL or whatever; but don't tell'em you don't follow sports or races at all. That flags ya as a "*loser*" right from the word *go!*

....

EPILOGUE

If ya wanna know more, then find out for yourself.

I'm hardly gunna waste my life writin' about Aussies.

....

www.ingramcontent.com/pod-product-compliance
Lightning Source LLC
Chambersburg PA
CBHW020904310526
45786CB00018B/1729